Great March towards Freedom

Maryam Rajavi's messages and speeches to the annual gatherings of Iranian Resistance at Ashraf 3 – Albania

July 2019

Great March towards Freedom

Maryam Rajavi's messages and speeches to the annual gatherings of Iranian Resistance at Ashraf 3 – Albania

ISBN: 978-2-491615-01-7

Published November 2019 by
National Council of Resistance of Iran
15, rue des Gords 95430 Auvers sur Oise- France

Table of Contents

Introduction

Iranian Resistance's annual gatherings at Ashraf 3

In addition to the gatherings at Ashraf 3, freedom loving Iranians held major rallies in five capitals of the world.

Beginning on July 11, the Iranian Resistance's gatherings this year were held for five days at Ashraf 3, the seat of the Iranian Resistance in Albania.

Ashraf 3 is an exceptional city. Twenty months before the gatherings, it was a bare piece of land. The city was built by the Mojahedin, with great effort.

During the five-day meetings and conferences, the freedom fighters of the main opposition People's Mojahedin Organization of Iran (PMOI/MEK) at Ashraf 3 hosted political dignitaries and international personalities as well as their countrymen and citizens from Europe, the U.S., Canada and Australia.

The annual gatherings of the Iranian Resistance at Ashraf 3 were kicked off by an international conference, entitled, "Iran policy and a credible alternative," featuring a number of prominent political personalities, international dignitaries, members of parliament, and experts from various countries who discussed the right policy vis-à-vis the clerical dictatorship in Iran and examined the most significant political and strategic issues in this regard.

On July 12, hundreds of personalities paid visit to a grand exhibition entitled, "120 years of struggle of the people of Iran for freedom." The tour to the exhibition was concluded by a conference where participants listened to speeches by Maryam Rajavi and a number of the guests as well as the testimonies of several former political prisoners.

The Free Iran gathering on July 13, featured speeches by Maryam Rajavi and dozens of political personalities, and officials from the United States and European countries. The Free Iran gathering was concluded by a brilliant concert held outdoors.

Sunday, July 14, featured an international conference on the role of women in the Iranian Resistance. Mrs. Rajavi attended and addressed this conference where a number of prominent women politicians, members of parliament and women's rights advocates also made speeches.

On the same day, an Arab-Islamic conference was held in solidarity with the people of Iran and the sole independent and democratic alternative. A number of dignitaries and delegations from Arab and Islamic countries participated and addressed this conference, which was entitled, "Overthrow of the mullahs' regime, imperative to end war and terrorism in the region." Personalities from Algeria, Tunisia, Bahrain, Jordan, Yemen, Lebanon, Morocco, Egypt and a delegation representing the Syrian opposition addressed this conference.

Another conference on Sunday, July 14, featured lawmakers and politicians from Europe who condemned the Iranian regime's terrorism and warmongering which have escalated during its last phase, and underlined their support for the Iranian Resistance.

The conference was moderated by Dr. Matthew Offord, senior member of the British House of Commons and president of the Parliamentary Group for a Free and Democratic Iran. He pointed out that the news media were referring to Ashraf 3 as "a beacon of hope."

The fifth day of the gatherings on July 15 was marked by another conference entitled, "Calling for Justice for the 1988 massacre; masterminds and perpetrators must face justice in international tribunals." Mrs. Rajavi attended and addressed the conference.

A number of political personalities, jurists, and human rights advocates were also in attendance and made speeches about the inhuman crimes of the mullahs' regime against the Iranian

people and Resistance, particularly the massacre of 30,000 political prisoners in 1988.

The speakers called for international investigations into the 1988 massacre and prosecution of the masterminds and perpetrators of this crime by international tribunals. A number of former PMOI political prisoners, including witnesses to the massacre of 30,000 political prisoners in 1988, testified at this conference on the crimes of the clerical regime.

This book has compiled the speeches made by Maryam Rajavi in the meetings and conferences held during the 2019 annual gatherings of the Iranian Resistance.

In addition to the gatherings at Ashraf 3, freedom loving Iranians held major rallies in five capitals of the world. Mrs. Rajavi sent video messages to the participants in these demonstrations. Excerpts of these messages are also included in this book.

Maryam Rajavi: We will take back Iran

Speech at the Free Iran Gathering at Ashraf 3

July 13, 2019

01

My fellow compatriots,

Honorable guests and distinguished dignitaries,

Ashraf 3 welcomes you all.

Twenty months ago, this was a piece of land with nothing on it.

At the hands of the Mojahedin, however, through their enormous efforts and hard work, Ashraf 3 was built and now stands tall.

But our final destination is Tehran, freed from the occupation of the mullahs.

The mullahs have devastated our homeland, but we will take it back and we will rebuild this most beautiful country.

> **Now, the mullahs' religious fascism has reached the end of the line and is struggling to survive a crisis leading to its overthrow.**
>
> **The economic devastation, elimination of over 70 percent of industrial capacity, a ruined banking sector, the monthly exodus of some $3billion worth of capital, and the ceaseless free fall of the value of the national currency, cannot be contained.**

We started this journey on June 20, 1981, when the Iranian Resistance's Leader Massoud Rajavi forged a deep-rooted and resolute resistance against the religious dictatorship of the mullahs.

He founded the National Council of Resistance of Iran (NCRI) and the National Liberation Army of Iran (NLA).

Now, Ashraf 3 stands tall along this long journey, a journey that has had many new beginnings and revivals throughout. On this path, we endured ten years of blood-drenched perseverance at the besieged Camp Ashraf and another four years full of determination at a slaughter house called Camp Liberty (in Iraq).

Now, this marks another chapter in a great march towards freedom, towards a free Iran, towards a glorious destination, of course after undergoing enormous suffering and dedicating a roaring river of the martyrs' blood.

On the first anniversary of the start of resistance against the mullahs, Massoud Rajavi said, "The triumph of our resistance will remove not only one of the greatest obstacles before contemporary revolutions, but in fact, the most important cause of their deviation and disintegration, namely the violation of the sacred parameters of freedom under various pretexts and excuses. The revival of the concept of freedom will resurrect humanity as well as defeated revolutions."

He said, "For a nation to appreciate her own freedom, she must ultimately free herself on her own."

He added, "Everyone can only free himself on his own from the yokes of coercion and oppression. And it is precisely for this reason that we are responsible to advance the goal of a general uprising for the freedom of our people and our country."

The mullahs' regime at an impasse

For the people of Iran, the forty years of the mullahs' rule is synonymous with an all-out massacre.

From several hundred executions every night in the notorious

Evin Prison and the massacre of political prisoners during the first decade of the regime's rule, to the massacre of the economy and production, environment, culture and art, and the Iranian civilization.

Now, the mullahs' religious fascism has reached the end of the line and is struggling to survive a crisis leading to its overthrow.

The economic devastation, elimination of over 70 percent of industrial capacity, a ruined banking sector, the monthly exodus of some $3billion worth of capital, and the ceaseless free fall of the value of the national currency, cannot be contained.

> **"Internationally, the mullahs are counting on inaction and tolerance on the part of the international community. Their calculation is that terrorist operations and warmongering in the region's countries will not cost them very much"**

The clerical regime is at an impasse. It neither has the capability to negotiate, abandon terrorism or stop meddling in the region, nor does it have any space to maneuver like it did during the appeasement era.

The regime's Supreme Leader Ali Khamenei calls negotiations with the U.S. poison and says it is doubly poisonous particularly with the current administration. Why? Because as he acknowledged, any change in the regime's behavior is tantamount to regime change and "every step back will bring with it an endless chain of subsequent retreats."

Where is the religious fascism headed?

Domestically, it is moving towards further contraction in its ranks more suppression of people in the broader society, and demonization and terrorism against the Iranian Resistance, which it views as its main threat and enemy; a resistance movement that calls for regime change to replace the rule of the vali-e faqih (absolute clerical rule) with the sovereignty and suffrage of the people; a resistance that has been fighting against this regime for four decades; a movement that as Khomeini's ousted successor (Ayatollah Hossein Ali Montazeri) conceded, cannot be annihilated through killings but is instead further strengthened.

Internationally, the mullahs are counting on inaction and tolerance on the part of the international community. Their calculation is that terrorist operations and warmongering in the region's countries will not cost them very much, at least until the next U.S. presidential election.

They say to themselves: let's wait another 16 months, and may be the U.S. would have another president from whom we can extract the same "super concessions" as we did in the nuclear deal!

At this point, I must recall that since November 24, 2013, throughout the negotiations, and both before and after the nuclear deal, the Iranian Resistance had been constantly warning against circumventing the six UN Security Council resolutions.

ایران

We particularly called for a complete halt to uranium enrichment, acceptance of the Additional Protocol, and the inspectors' unhindered access to all IRGC centers and other regime suspect sites.

In April 2015, before the nuclear accord was signed, I declared at a French Senate meeting that, "The experience of the Iranian Resistance shows that the mullahs only understand the language of force and firmness." And I stressed, "The time has come for major powers to stop appeasing and giving concessions to the murderous religious tyranny, the central banker of terrorism, and the world's record holder of executions, and to recognize the right of the people of Iran for resistance and freedom."

> **Internationally, the mullahs are counting on inaction and tolerance on the part of the international community. Their calculation is that terrorist operations and warmongering in the region's countries will not cost them very much, at least until the next U.S. presidential election.**

On the day of the agreement, on July 14, 2015, we said again, "An agreement that overlooks the human rights of the Iranian people and fails to emphasize and acknowledge them, will only encourage further suppression and incessant executions on the part of this regime. It will also trample upon the rights of the people of Iran, the Universal Declaration of Human Rights, and the UN Charter… because the people of Iran have been the main victims of this ominous nuclear program."

A glance at recent developments

Now, let us review the events that have transpired over the past two months:

On May 29, 2019, in an implicit reference to the terrorist operations in Fujairah (UAE), Saudi Arabia and Iraq, Khamenei said, “If (our) bargaining chips and leverage are used properly, U.S. pressure would either dwindle or cease. But if we are deceived by the American “invitations to talk” and do not use our levers of pressure… (our) loss is inevitable.”

As for increasing their uranium enrichment to a level beyond the permissible limits, he made the following threat, “We will not stop at that level. In the next stage, we will use other levers of pressure, if necessary.”

Indeed, the attack on the Japanese oil tanker at exactly the time when the Prime Minister of Japan was in Tehran for mediations and the downing of a U.S. drone are among the pressure tactics and instruments mentioned by Khamenei. The regime’s President Hassan Rouhani curried favor (with the IRGC) and said that he kisses the hands of the involved Revolutionary Guards [commanders and officers].

Just recently, the regime declared that it had boosted its uranium enrichment to 4.5% and threatened to take the next steps.

Additionally, last week, Rouhani tried to blackmail and humiliate European countries by saying, “We will revert the reactor in Arak back to its previous condition, the very conditions that you used to say were dangerous because of their capacity to produce plutonium.”

Indeed, in view of such threats, what can we make of their ridiculous claims that the religious fascism considers nuclear weapons to be forbidden and Khamenei has issued a fatwa in this regard? What happened to those claims? Didn't they simply make a mockery of the media and public opinion using those claims?

And the game of hide and seek continues…

The regime's schisms and instability

Clearly, the regime is fueling tensions in a bid to push back against the international community. They foment turmoil and chaos to hide their fear of being overthrown. They want firmness to be replaced with the policy of appeasement. And they want to allay fears and anxiety of their Bassij forces and Revolutionary Guards and to preserve their internal balance and equilibrium.

A former Rouhani advisor has said that when it comes to determining foreign policy within the regime, the two schools of "confrontation" or "engagement" are facing off against each other. In a bid to consolidate power, in a speech on May 22, Khamenei ordered his audience to "set the stage for the creation of a young, Hezbollahi government."

However, the reality is that schism and instability are among the signs that the regime is in its final chapter. The clerical regime is not going to find a way out of its inevitable downfall.

Baptizing the godfather of terrorism

In line with the policy of appeasing the religious fascism over the past three decades, regime apologists turned a blind eye to its crimes committed both within Iran and abroad. They baptized the central banker and the greatest sponsor and godfather of international terrorism.

> **"As the Iranian Resistance said from the outset, fighting against this regime is equivalent to seeking peace because it eliminates the source of war and turmoil."**

Instead of the regime, they targeted its arch-nemesis, namely the Iranian Resistance, leveling fictitious accusations against it. They blacklisted the Mojahedin instead of Khamenei's network, and the National Liberation Army of Iran instead the Islamic Revolutionary Guard Corps (IRGC).

Of course, we proudly prevailed in more than 20 courts. They did not find even a single piece of incriminating evidence against the MEK. This history is reminiscent of the ancient Iranian myth where the hero Siavash safely passes through flames of accusations against him.

Velayat-e Faqih, the source of war

Now the obscuring curtains are being pulled away one by one. Everyone can clearly see that the source of war and warmongering is the velayat-e faqih regime. As the Iranian Resistance said from the outset, fighting against this regime is equivalent to seeking peace because it eliminates the source of war and turmoil.

The spin doctors of the clerical regime used to claim that if the mullahs were to be overthrown, Iran would experience war, turmoil and secessions. Now, everyone can see that so long as this regime remains in place, war and crises will continue and intensify in the region. Therefore, anyone who seeks freedom for Iran, anyone who wants to save Iran from destruction and chaos, anyone who wants global and regional peace and stability, must rise up to demand the overthrow of the mullahs' regime.

The big ruse created by proponents of appeasement

The proponents of appeasement seek to paint the policy of firmness against the regime as being tantamount to warmongering. But this is a big ruse and deception. Giving the mullahs any more chances will only end up emboldening them.

Their path must be blocked. Albania is an example in this regard.

Last December, in the wake of the Iranian regime and its embassy's terrorist schemes in this country, the government of Albania expelled the mullahs' ambassador and their Intelligence Ministry station chief and terrorist. Subsequently, the U.S. President praised the efforts of the government of Albania in standing up to the regime and confronting its destabilizing activities to silence its opponents. This was to signal to the Iranian regime that its terrorist activities in Europe and all around the world would have serious consequences.

The essential point is that the clerical regime sees that contrary to the past, each of its actions carry serious repercussions.

Yes, a regime whose crimes and warmongering are increasingly exposed on a daily basis must anticipate many more consequences.

Historical mission of the Resistance, removing the velayat-e faqih's veil of fear

After developing a deep understanding about the nature of the ruling theocracy, the Iranian Resistance has been insisting for four decades that the regime is incapable of reform and therefore it is imperative to overthrow and change it. The NCRI has been underscoring the threat this regime poses to regional and global peace and tranquility, and has called for the imposition of comprehensive sanctions on the religious fascism ruling Iran.

Indeed, if the reactionary nature of Khomeini and his mullahs

had not been exposed;

If the Mojahedin had not endured suffering and made the ultimate sacrifice in the fight against the mullahs' IRGC and Gestapo-like intelligence services;

If they had not forced Khomeini to accept the ceasefire in the Iran-Iraq war;

If the Mojahedin had not insisted on their stance at the cost of a massacre;

If they had not remained steadfast in Ashraf and Liberty;

If the mullahs' regime had not been condemned 65 times by the United Nations for its human rights violations;

And if the Iranian Resistance had not published its informative books and evidence;

If it had not exposed the IRGC's terrorism, especially the list of 32,000 mercenaries of the Quds Force in Iraq;

If it had not exposed the regime's secret nuclear projects and facilities in Natanz and Arak;

And if it had not awakened and alerted the world about the mullahs' clandestine bomb making program with over 100 accurate and documented disclosures over quarter of a century;

Today, the situation would have been radically different, and the mullahs, equipped with nuclear weapons, would have created and solidified the empire and Caliphate they have long intended to establish.

Yes, the Iranian people and Resistance have paid the necessary and full price. Otherwise, the groundwork for their terrorist designation would never have been created.

Yes, the Iranian Resistance under the leadership of Massoud Rajavi, has accomplished its historic mission, breaking the atmosphere of fear and intimidation created by the velayat-e faqih and their criminal Revolutionary Guard Corps. It has thus left no future for the mullahs' evil caliphate.

The clerical regime's overthrow is the definite solution

The definitive, ultimate and indisputable solution is the overthrow of the religious dictatorship in its entirety at the hands of the people of Iran and their Resistance.

Those who benefit from the perpetuation of this regime used to give bogus promises of reform and moderation in the past, and today, they beat the drums of demonization and disseminate fake news against the Mojahedin and the Iranian Resistance.

> **"After developing a deep understanding about the nature of the ruling theocracy, the Iranian Resistance has been insisting for four decades that the regime is incapable of reform and therefore it is imperative to overthrow and change it"**

They want to play the role of the regime's saviors. Over the past year alone, 11,500 completely fake and deceptive regime twitter accounts have been closed.

They want to say that there is no alternative to the regime and everyone would benefit from tolerating the mullahs.

But can they stop the wheels of history from turning? Can they reverse the progress of history? Never!

The mullahs' regime and those backing it in its fight against the people of Iran, keep repeating that the Iranian Resistance does not enjoy any support inside Iran.

And we say and reiterate that if the regime's claims are true, why does it not allow us to hold peaceful gatherings and demonstrations across Iran for one single day and only one day?

Of course, the regime has never allowed this and will never do so. Why? Because the mullahs are fully aware that they will be swiftly swept away from power.

Resistance is the only benchmark under repression

Everyone knows that under absolute repression and intimidation, and as long as there is no chance for gatherings, demonstrations, opinion polls, and free elections, the only genuine benchmark (of legitimacy) is resistance. Nothing else is equally essential or relevant.

It is with the yardstick of resistance that one can measure the level of support for this movement.

They can measure it by looking at the resolve of PMOI

freedom fighters, the struggle waged by units of rebellion, and the efforts and rallies of exiled Iranians and supporters of the Iranian Resistance who cry out, "We will take back Iran."

Units of rebellion

The creation and spread of units of rebellion and resistance councils has marked a major breakthrough, demonstrating the rightfulness and precision of this strategy during the December 2017-January 2018 uprising and subsequent developments.

This Resistance has been able to expand and organize its network inside Iran despite the pervasive repression. This is how Ashraf has been replicated in society and among the people of Iran.

From a strategic standpoint, the units of rebellion are the answer to a regime that is incapable of reform and will not fall under its own weight. Rather, it can and must be overthrown through the struggle of the Mojahedin, the units of rebellion and the people of Iran.

In its attempts to confront units of rebellion, the regime has recently set up new patrols called "neighborhood patrols" and "Razaviyoun." It has even reassigned anti-vice patrols in many parts of the country to focus on arresting members of these rebellion units.

Earlier this year, Mahmoud Alavi, the Minister of Intelligence, announced that 116 PMOI teams have been arrested. Then, the director general of intelligence in East Azerbaijan Province said the regime had arrested and confronted 110 persons with ties to the Mojahedin in that province alone. They subsequently issued

Stephen
Harper

death sentences and lengthy prison terms.

But the enemy can neither succeed in breaking the morale of resistance forces in prisons nor is it able to thwart the resistance movement and the units of rebellion in cities.

Yes, every young man or woman yearning for freedom and justice is a potential or de facto rebel. A unit of rebellion wrote from Tabriz: We will stand until the end and will get through all the ups and downs. Victory is ours and the dawn is looming.

113 years ago, after the heroism and sacrifice of Sattar Khan and his Mojahedin in Tabriz in the northwest, the biggest rebellious city at the time, the Mojahedin advanced from Rasht in the north and Isfahan in the center and conquered Tehran. May this time, too, the people of Iran conquer Tehran with their units of rebellion and the great Army of Freedom, liberating the entire country from the mullahs' occupation.

The Land of Lion and Sun embracing freedom

Today, two sides are facing off against each other over the fate of Iran. On the one side is a deadlocked regime, and on the other is a nation and its Resistance fighting for freedom.

Yes, there is an alternative that wants to reach the destination of freedom through units of rebellion, rebellious cities and the Army of Freedom. This alternative is capable of establishing a democratic and pluralist republic based on the separation of religion and state, gender equality, autonomy of Iran's ethnic groups, and a non-nuclear Iran.

> **From a strategic standpoint, the units of rebellion are the answer to a regime that is incapable of reform and will not fall under its own weight. Rather, it can and must be overthrown through the struggle of the Mojahedin, the units of rebellion and the people of Iran.**

The National Council of Resistance of Iran has concrete plans and platforms. Thanks to its organization and cohesiveness, the NCRI can replace the regime and is able to ensure a peaceful transition of power to the Iranian people's elected representatives.

Yes, the day is not far when Iran, the Land of Lion and Sun, will embrace freedom.

We are determined to create a new future, a new plan devoid of tyranny, reactionary thought, duplicity and discrimination. A new design for a free and prosperous Iran.

So, we will sing in unison as we march toward victory: we will take back Iran and we will build a new homeland.

Yes, indeed, we will take back Iran.

Maryam Rajavi: Iranian people and history are forging ahead on the path towards certain victory

Speech at the exhibition of

the Iranian people's 120 years of

struggle for freedom

Ashraf 3

July 12, 2019

02

Dear friends,

It is a great pleasure for me to welcome you to Ashraf 3. Once again, I would like to thank you for your efforts in support of Ashrafis and the Iranian Resistance. Efforts that finally led to the collective and safe relocation of the Mojahedin (PMOI/MEK). This was a great accomplishment in which you all played a part.

The mullahs and the Islamic Revolutionary Guard Corps (IRGC) sought to massacre these trailblazers for freedom, these freedom fighters. However, we defeated their quest for annihilation. This was but one of the chapters in the struggle for a free Iran. And I am confident that you will continue your efforts, standing with the Ashrafis until the day we reach Tehran and establish a free and democratic Iran.

Today in Ashraf 3, we have gathered at a location that features an Exhibition depicting 120 years of the Iranian people's struggle for freedom. A struggle with countless ups and downs, with many defeats and triumphs, animated by tears and smiles of an enchained nation oppressed by two dictatorships, the previous monarchy and then a religious tyrannical regime. But we are forging ahead on the path towards certain victory.

We have consistently broken new ground and advanced through firing squads, massacres, missile attacks, bombardments and terrorist designations, for the removal of which you all stood by our side.

Time and again, flames were set to burn us down, but we rose up again like a phoenix from ashes. We successfully prevailed over malicious hostilities, demonization campaigns and unbridled terrorism. The ruling mullahs in Iran want to claim that there is no viable alternative and that the People's Mojahedin Organization of Iran (PMOI/MEK) lacks a social base and has no support.

But thanks to our own and our people's perseverance, history has nothing but scorn for the mullahs.

The missing link in the Iranian people's 120-year struggle

Through their 120-year-long struggle, our people have found, one by one, the missing links for achieving definite victory, while paying the heaviest possible price along the way.

One of the missing links in previous movements of the Iranian people was a coherent organization and an organized struggle, coupled with a determined and battle-hardened force prepared to make any sacrifice necessary. As a result, the people's previous struggles did not succeed despite all their sacrifices. And, today, Ashraf 3 embodies the organized resistance of the people of Iran for freedom.

> **"Iran's ruling mullahs want to claim that there is no viable alternative and that the People's Mojahedin Organization lacks a social base and has no support. But thanks to our own and our people's perseverance, history has nothing but scorn for the mullahs."**

As I studied portions of this exhibition, even though I have personally been involved in all the moments of this resistance with all its peaks and valleys for more than 40 years, I could not help but be in awe of the authenticity of these women and men and the magnificence of this resistance on the one hand, and on

exhibition of the Iranian people's 120 years of struggle for freedom

Ashraf 3 -Albania

the other hand be shocked by the crimes of the mullahs' regime against the best and brightest among the people of Iran.

Time does not permit me to best convey the profound impact of every scene. You will see it for yourselves. On the one hand are excessive crimes and on the other, great sacrifices, faith and a legendary resistance by pioneers of the Iranian nation, which is truly remarkable.

Of course, this exhibition is just a snapshot of the history of the Iranian people's struggle for freedom.

In the beginning of the 20th century, during the Constitutional Revolution, our nation managed to push aside the absolute monarchical dictatorship. But in the absence of democratic structures and institutions, despotism re-emerged in less than 15 years. Lacking leadership and organization, freedom lovers were

“In the beginning of the 20th century, during the Constitutional Revolution, our nation managed to push aside the absolute monarchical dictatorship. But in the absence of democratic structures and institutions, despotism re-emerged in less than 15 years.”

suppressed. Reza Khan staged a coup and established another dictatorship.

Thirty years later, in 1951, Dr. Mohammad Mossadeq, the leader of the oil nationalization movement, formed the first and only truly nationalist and democratic government in Iran. In less than 2.5 years, however, his government was toppled through a coup d'etat. Mossadeq was imprisoned, and his Foreign Minister, Hossein Fatemi, was executed.

And the Shah's hideous dictatorship lasted for another 25 years in Iran.

If Mossadeq had the chance to institutionalize a democratic tradition in Iran, the situation would have been completely different today both in Iran and in the region. And beyond a shadow of a doubt, there would have been no space for fundamentalism and extremism.

The Shah's true crown prince was Khomeini. The single-party monarchic dictatorship of the Shah did away with all the traditional parties. So, in the absence of basic freedoms and political parties, no one remained on the scene except Khomeini.

The Shah executed or imprisoned the leaders of the Mojahedin and all the progressive forces, empowering Khomeini, a religious authority in exile, to exploit the Iranian people's uprisings and revolution.

In fact, he hijacked the Iranian people's revolution and from the outset established his religious dictatorship, which he referred to as the absolute rule of the jurisprudent. Despite all the crimes and massacres he committed, Khomeini failed to extinguish the flames of freedom.

Freedom, the goal of the anti-monarchic revolution

With the rallying cry of freedom and under the leadership of Massoud Rajavi, who had just been released from prison after our people's uprisings (in 1979), the People's Mojahedin Organization of Iran (PMOI/MEK) hoisted the banner of struggle against religious dictatorship since the beginning. Massoud

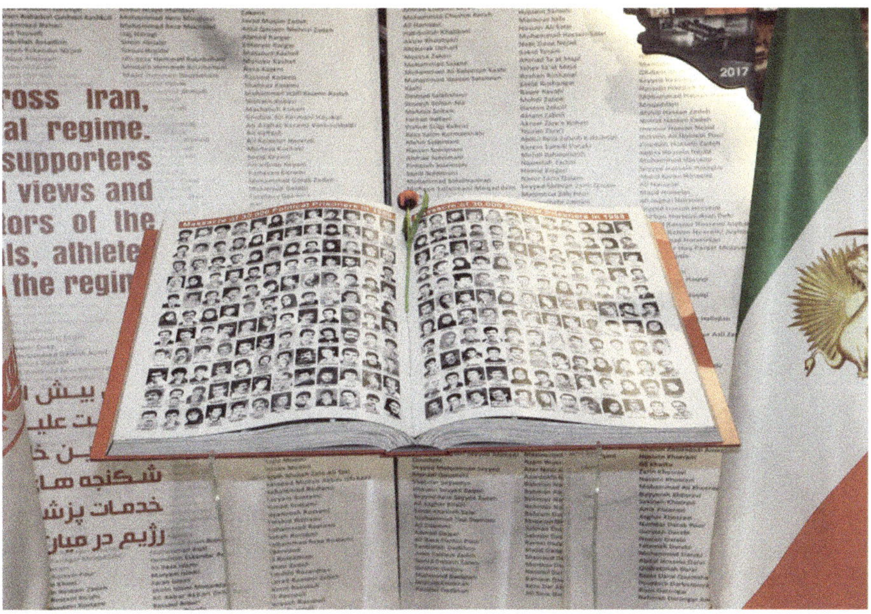
ross Iran,
al regime.
supporters
views and
tors of the
ls, athlete
the regim
2017

did not allow Khomeini to hide his bloodthirsty image behind the mask of religion, and he did not let Khomeini establish an eternal rule for his Satanic Caliphate under the banner of Islam. Employing the rallying cries of peace and freedom, he did not let Khomeini continue his unjust eight-year war with Iraq.

With the motto of "conquering Quds (Jerusalem) via Karbala" and Iraq, Khomeini's war left one million dead and an additional million maimed and wounded on the Iranian side alone, along with 4 million people displaced, $1 trillion worth of damages and 50 towns burnt to the ground.

> **“If Mossadeq had the chance to institutionalize a democratic tradition in Iran, the situation would have been completely different today in Iran and in the region.”**

Massoud established the National Council of Resistance of Iran in 1981, and six years later, he founded the National Liberation Army of Iran. Early on, shortly after Khomeini returned to Iran, he told Massoud during a meeting in Tehran: "You are young and young people listen to you. Write down a few sentences and say that those who are not religious are not entitled to engage in political activities. And then all paths will be open to you." Massoud responded by saying that he could not do so "because the Iranian people's revolution pursued freedom, and in our view, Islam is a religion of freedom."

So, Khomeini quickly discovered that the Mojahedin would not abandon their goals and their conviction in freedom in order to score political ranks or positions.

40 years of struggle between autocracy and liberty

Over the past 40 years, 120,000 people have given their lives for the cause of freedom. That includes the 30,000 people who were massacred in 1988 for insisting on their political identity as members of the Mojahedin. Another half-a-million people were arrested and viciously tortured.

They forced our imprisoned sisters to remain in a squatted position for days and weeks in a container called "the cage" in an attempt to force them to surrender. Some of those prisoners, who endured this form of torture for months, are here today. The regime employed other vicious torture methods, including the torture of a mother in front of her child and vice versa, and hanging the prisoner from the ceiling. But despite all these tortures, they could not break their spirits.

This is how the Resistance continued, grew and expanded to Ashraf and Liberty. The mullahs continued their crimes against Ashraf and Liberty through the declaration of 22 deadlines in 10 years, through a medical blockade, through psychological torture using over 300 loudspeakers blaring into Ashraf for two years, and through 29 ground and aerial attacks, using armored vehicles and missile launchers, including the commission of seven bloodbaths and massacres. This was the price that every member of the Mojahedin has paid with his/her life and emotions.

If you ask any one of them, they will tell you that their perseverance was based on three things:

First, making a conscious choice and decision to pursue the

path of God and the people, which is the path of history and evolution;

Second, choosing to pursue the cause of the Iranian people's freedom, which was also a conscious choice demanding a very heavy toll;

And finally, having a suitable setting for the realization of this goal, namely the People's Mojahedin Organization of Iran, which for the past 40 years the mullahs have mobilized all their evil powers to destroy.

Dear friends,

The political scene of the past 40 years in Iran has been a battleground for a conflict between autocracy and liberty pioneered by the Mojahedin. From the country's north to the south, there is not a single city in Iran that has not been colored by the blood of the Mojahedin.

Ashraf has risen up, proud and powerful

But today, we have reached a historic turning point. An Ashraf which has once again risen up, proud and powerful, shining bright at the zenith of this Resistance.

This Ashraf has been replicated 1000 times in the form of resistance units all over Iran. And a volatile society which is no longer willing to put up with the mullahs, yearning to overthrow them.

On the opposite side, there is a crisis-riddled regime engulfed in warmongering and terrorism, facing international sanctions and standing on its last leg. But the Iranian people and history are forging ahead on the road to certain victory.

On this path, the PMOI/MEK, whose Central Council is made up of 1,000 heroines, is a national treasure for the people of Iran. Far beyond being a mere political organization, it is the focal point for their hopes and aspirations to obtain freedom and democracy.

There is no doubt that freedom will prevail over dictatorship. The Iranian people's moment of liberation is fast approaching.

Maryam Rajavi: Women's progress in the Resistance movement is beholden to a ceaseless battle against reactionary and exploitative thinking

Speech to the international conference at Ashraf 3 on women's leadership in the Iranian Resistance

July 14, 2019

03

Greetings to my dear sisters from Albania, European countries, the United States, Canada, Australia, Asia and Arab countries who are attending this conference.

I would also like to salute my dear sisters, members of the Iranian Resistance's big family. Welcome to Ashraf 3.

And I hail members of the Central Council of the People's Mojahedin Organization of Iran (PMOI/MEK), the majority of whom are participating in this gathering.

This gathering usually takes place on the International Women's Day, but any time that women come together to discuss their mission for freedom and equality and for emancipation of society in general that is a time day belongs to women.

This is particularly true for the women of Iran because they are defying and resisting against a fundamentalist and reactionary regime, whose most distinctive feature is misogyny.

> **"The regime which took over in 1979, however, was misogynous and theocratic and retarded Iranian women's progress."**

Before the current regime seized power in Iran, women participated in uprisings in large numbers. This indicated a transformation in the status of women and their role in the democratic struggle. Women's widespread participation in the anti-monarchic revolution had significant precedent in Iranian women's past struggles. Specifically, in the 1970s, women actively participated in the revolutionary struggle against the Shah. Some of the most prominent pioneers were Fatemeh

Amini, Marzieh Uskowi, Azam Rouhi Ahangaran and Ashraf Rajavi. They made great sacrifices to pave the way for the revolution.

The regime which took over in 1979, however, was misogynous and theocratic and reversed the progress made by Iranian women.

I remember those days quite well. It seemed like a showdown between two opposing forces. The mullahs' enmity against women, and the latter's disdain for and distrust in the new regime, started the very day that Khomeini took power.

As soon as the mullahs hijacked the revolution, they began their clampdown on women with the motto of "either the veil or a slap in the face."

At the same time, women also started their resistance against this regime, which has continued to this day.

I would like to briefly review the status of Iranian women from a few different angles:

Misogyny is the essence and driving force of the regime's suppression of society in general

As for political participation, I must say that women have no role in the ruling regime and in its decision making at any level of its hierarchy.

Another issue is depriving women of their personal and social freedoms and their right to freedom of choice. Women have been deprived of their rights to travel, marry and have a private life, choose their occupation, and the most pervasive of all, their free choice of clothing.

Another issue is the existence of hideous inequalities and discriminations against women under the rule of the clerical regime.

Drastic inequalities in job opportunities, in wages, in families, in education, in testimony before a court, in having access to medical services and insurance, in their share of inheritance, in access to sports fields and stadiums, and a long list of denial of rights in every realm.

> **"A deeper look into the reason for the mullahs' savagery towards women reveals that misogyny is the driving force and the essence of the regime's suppression of society in general."**

Such discrimination in any society, at any juncture in history, would mean subjugation of the people, suppression, plundering and deprivation of political rights.

Another issue is promoting violence against women.

Women of Iran do not feel safe anywhere, not at the work place, not when they commute in the streets, and not even among their families. The regime enforces this clampdown through countless number of patrols, security forces and police tasked with offending, insulting and arresting women.

Inhumane treatment of women in prisons is common practice. Since Hassan Rouhani became president, some 90 women have been hanged.

A deeper look into the reasons behind the mullahs' savagery towards women reveals that misogyny is the driving force and the essence of the regime's suppression of society in general.

Women, the main victims of rampant poverty and destitution in Iran

I must also underline the rampant poverty and destitution in today's Iran, the primary victims of which are women.

Over 62 percent of women above 10 years old are housewives. Those who have a job are considered the world's cheapest work force. Women make up half of the workers of brick kilns in Iran.

The average economic participation of women in the Middle East is 22 percent. But this rate is only 12 percent in the cities of Iran. This rate has not changed for over five decades.

In reviewing the status of 200 countries, the International Labor Organization announced that Iran is among the six countries at the bottom of the list, namely among the war-stricken and shattered countries such as Syria and Iraq.

You must have heard the spin doctors of the regime claiming that if the mullahs were to be overthrown, Iran would experience chaos and disaster. This is while Iranian women are currently living in conditions reminiscent of and even worse than war-torn countries; they are suffering from poverty, destitution, unemployment and homelessness.

Look at the meager wages of young female workers and their agonizing work environments.

Young women with Bachelor's or Master's degrees are working for salaries equivalent to 10 to 20 dollars a month.

In fact, women are not only cheap laborers in Iran's job market but also subjected to horribly oppressive working conditions.

We believe that the common answer to all these problems is freedom and equality. Not just equality and not just freedom. But both freedom and equality, together. This is the answer for the liberation of women. This is why I have always emphasized that women not only will free themselves but also their societies at large.

This is our mission and we are determined to accomplish it.

Women at the forefront of the struggle against the mullahs' theocratic rule

A few minutes ago, I pointed to women's widespread participation in the struggle against two dictatorships. Let me add that they have always been at the forefront of the struggle since the outset of the mullahs' theocratic rule, and more significantly, they have been the trailblazers and leaders of this struggle.

Those days, women faced more difficulties than men in joining the democratic struggle. Young Muslim women, in particular, faced greater problems because before the founding of the People's Mojahedin Organization of Iran (PMOI/EMK) there was no precedent for Muslim women in struggle against dictatorship. The PMOI broke a taboo.

Later on, under the leadership of Massoud Rajavi, throngs of women nationwide joined the PMOI's struggle against Khomeini, as the regime's supreme leader, and against reactionary and fundamentalist Islam.

They wanted freedom, equality and a democratic Islam. But the regime continued to impose more restrictions and apply greater pressure on women and increasingly deprived them of their rights.

The history of struggle in the past four decades against religious dictatorship is notable because of the leading role of PMOI women.

These days, you have seen an exhibition (at Ashraf 3) that displays parts of the history of the Iranian people's resistance over the past 40 years. It reminds us of the torturous and blood-soaked path paved by women of the Iranian Resistance. You saw the images showing cages where prisoners were detained. Some of the women held in these cages for a long time are now sitting here among you.

You have seen images of the torture chambers called residential units, where female prisoners were sadistically mistreated and harassed 24 hours a day.

You can see the survivors of the 1988 massacre.

In this gathering, you can see those who have endured such horrible conditions and are now proudly fulfilling their duties in our struggle.

Many books have been written about these women's struggle and resistance in the mullahs' torture chambers, about some of the tens of thousands of women tortured and executed over the past 40 years, from Fatemeh Mesbah, only 13, to Mother Zakeri, 70. Nevertheless, the story of these women's resistance still remains an untold story.

The story of enduring vicious torture, resisting the barbaric actions of interrogators and the Revolutionary Guards, the resistance to preserve a collective fighting spirit in prison, making the effort to rejoin the PMOI, and the attempt to form new resistance cells are all part of the legendary perseverance of these women.

All of these were epics of perseverance of these women.

These women have proven their capabilities in the military field as well.

Another chapter of this struggle was overcoming the hardships and complexities related to the presence of women in the ranks of an army fighting the enemy, the formation of combat units, being trained and assuming commanding roles, fighting against all obstacles in camps Ashraf and Liberty and continuing to resist for 14 years.

> **Issues like poverty and discrimination, homeless children and citizens, environmental disasters, and most importantly, political and social participation of all individuals, the right to the freedom of choice, and of course, eliminating gender discrimination.**

WOMEN FORCE FOR CHANGE

1,000 pioneering women in the PMOI Central Council

Now, you can see 1,000 pioneering women in Ashraf 3, who have come here from different cities of Iran, and who have studied at universities in the U.S., Europe and Iran. Some gave up their jobs and families for freedom of their people and country and have joined the Mojahedin. What you see here are three generations of women sitting side by side. In fact, the most senior body that is leading this movement is made up of only PMOI women.

This accomplishment is the fruit of the path the Mojahedin have paved from the beginning under the leadership of Massoud Rajavi with conviction in freedom and equality.

I should point out that two months after Khomeini took power, the Mojahedin issued a 15-point declaration explaining their expectations from the new regime. In article 6 of this declaration, they have reiterated the need "to respect all political and social rights of women" and specifically, they stressed "equal pay for equal work" for female workers.

A few months later, when Massoud ran for the presidential elections, he offered a ten-point plan which started with the formation of councils with the participation of people to run the country's affairs. Again, the seventh article of this plan emphasized the equality of women and men.

There were other articles on the rights of ethnic groups, freedom of parties, freedom of opinion, freedom of the press, and equality of Shiites and Sunnis which were widely embraced by women and youth, by ethnic groups and followers of religions other than Islam. Virtually all political groups and parties endorsed the plan. This is what terrified Khomeini and compelled him to make a disgraceful decision against his own promise which removed Massoud from the list of candidates.

> **"Women believe that it is their duty to save Iran from dictatorship, poverty and regression, to save millions of hungry and homeless children, to save so many unfortunate women whose lives have been tainted with misery."**

In such a torturous struggle, there was a generation of young women and girls who became increasingly informed every day and widely participated in the anti-fundamentalist struggle and in the fight for freedom and equality.

One of the most important chapters in this brilliant struggle was the existence of young women, young teenagers who waged the strongest resistance against the revolutionary guards and torturers. Among them were heroines like Homeira Eshraq, Zahra and Kobra Ebrahimian and Sorayya Abolfathi. Their names are etched in the history of women's struggle forever.

Their first encounters with politics and democratic struggle happened when they first got to know Massoud Rajavi and believed in his cause which was freedom. Every one of them became a pioneer on this path. Today, young women are joining the resistance units and continuing their path. Therefore, when we speak of members of the PMOI's Central Council, we are talking about women who have:

Firstly, conquered prisons and opened their way into battle fields.

Secondly, they have opened their way in the overall struggle by fighting two horrific ideologies. One of them is the ideology of gender discrimination, and the other the ideology of negative individuality.

I deliberately use the word negative, to distinguish between this subjugating ideology and evolutionary or positive individuality which leads to the spiritual growth of human beings.

These women have shouldered a heavy responsibility. They have chosen to hold firm to their commitment in every defeat or victory, and in all the trials and tribulations.

The liberation of society requires women's leadership and acceptance of responsibility

The imperative that motivates these women to accept responsibility and lead the movement, is the liberation of Iranian society. This is our responsibility. We must respond to the most serious sufferings and challenges in our communities: These include fighting poverty and discrimination, helping homeless children and citizens, combating environmental disasters, and most importantly, defending political and social participation of all individuals, the right to freedom of choice, and of course, eliminating gender discrimination.

All of these are our responsibilities.

> **“Iran’s enlightened women and rebellious girls inspired by the 1,000 women of Ashraf, are following the tradition of an emancipating struggle.”**

I must emphasize that equality and emancipation of women would be realistic only when accompanied by the emancipation of men.

This is the achievement of our movement, namely human growth and advancement of pioneering men who have rebelled against gender discrimination and patriarchy to build truly equal relationships. And on this path, they have emancipated themselves.

If our movement did not profoundly reject exploitation and all of its political, social, theoretical, and cultural components, women could not have held such positions within it for long.

Women’s advancement in the resistance movement is before anything else indebted to a consistent struggle against reactionary and exploitative thinking.

It is generally opined that women are second-class citizens and incapable of doing many things. This mindset is as old as the history of mankind.

But the women of this resistance have defied this mindset and are continuing to resist against it. The more these women shed negative individualism, and improve upon their interactions, the more efficient and capable they become in shouldering more responsibilities and paving the way for their advancement.

This means moving away from living in seclusion and entering social life, which is the product of human evolution at the highest levels of human relationships that requires constant struggle.

Today, the women of Iran are the answer to the overthrow of the religious dictatorship, and tomorrow they will herald peace and rebuildings

Women can and must lead and have a pioneering role along this path.

This is why the women of Iran are capable of overthrowing the religious dictatorship today and will herald peace and rebuilding in the future.

Fortunately, today, the emancipating message of the PMOI, and specifically the message of gender equality, has been embraced by young women and men in cities across Iran.

The resistance units have expanded over the past two years. Women in the Iranian resistance have acted as the role model for them.

A young woman from Khorramabad wrote: "I am a leaf on the PMOI's robust tree. I'm alive, and I fight. I am a Mojahed, therefore I am."

And these are the words of a woman by the name of Mina, also a member of a resistance unit: "I dream about blossoming of the flowers of my hope and a voice that tells me, 'Although the night is dark, be confident that the dawn is near.' In the depths of darkness, I am dreaming of becoming a butterfly."

These enlightened and brave young women and men have been and continue to be inspired by four decades of sacrifice and perseverance of the PMOI. For them, the Mojahedin's conviction in, and adherence to, the cause of freedom and equality is a living example which guides them in the struggle against the ruling tyrannical regime.

At this point, I would like to salute Iran's political prisoners especially my sisters who have been resisting and defying the regime in Khamenei's jails in various cities.

In addition to opposition to dictatorship, they have committed the "unforgivable crime" of being a rebellious woman.

To be a woman and not surrender, to be a woman and persevere in struggle, to be a woman and instead of thinking about yourself, think about the liberation of a people in chains, this is something that has driven the mullahs insane.

And finally, please allow me to address my sisters in Iran, especially the conscious young women who are fed up with the intolerable circumstances prevailing in Iran.

The present circumstances are extraordinary. The regime is at an impasse. Society is like embers beneath the ashes. The economy is totally paralyzed.

The clerical regime is working day and night to force Iranian women into submission.

But Iran's enlightened women and rebellious girls inspired by the 1,000 women of Ashraf, are following the tradition of an emancipating struggle. This is a role model devoid of all gender-based discriminations in outlook, standards, mentalities and values. This is a model according to which women are arisen, decisive, and capable of having an impact and opening the way. Women believe that the political fate of their country and society is equal to their own fate.

They believe that it is their duty to save Iran from dictatorship, poverty and regression, to save millions of hungry and homeless children, to save so many unfortunate women whose lives have been tainted with misery.

This is how enlightened and rebellious women go into the battle fields of emancipation. This is how they realize gender equality.

I thank you all very much.

> “To be a woman and not surrender, to be a woman and persevere in struggle, to be a woman and instead of thinking about yourself, think about the liberation of a people in chains, this is something that has driven the mullahs insane.”

Maryam Rajavi: The 1988 massacre is tied to Iran's freedom and future

Speech at the conference of Calling for Justice for the 1988 Massacre – Ashraf3

July 12, 2019

04

I salute you all.

And I greet you sisters and brothers, especially the more than 900 former political prisoners (among the residents of Ashraf3) who have been tortured by the dictatorships of the Shah and Khomeini, many of whom are here today.

We are approaching the 31st anniversary of the martyrdom of 30,000 political prisoners massacred as a result of Khomeini's fatwa (religious decree) for the "crime" of remaining loyal to their pledge of being a "Mojahed" and to their ideal, which is freedom of the people of Iran.

Thousands of salutes to those young souls, lovers of freedom and beauty, those clear reflections of the Iranian people's aspirations.

(Translation of a piece of Persian Poetry)
Although those friends do not remember me
I remember them a thousand times
Although a hundred rivers of tears flow from my eyes
I hold dear their living memories which cultivated numerous gardens

The victims of the 1988 massacre are the valiant conscience of Iran's history. They are the gem of honesty, sacrifice and loyalty kept dear in the heart of our nation whose true existence is indebted to it.

In the heat of this carnage, in one of the wards of the Prison of Ahvaz, two blood-thirsty mullahs by the names of Jazayeri and Abdollahi said, "You must make up your mind. Khomeini is on one side and Massoud Rajavi is on the other. Which side are you on?"

At the end of the hall, a young woman cried out, "Long live

Massoud, down with Khomeini." She was Sakineh Delfi, 26, a heroine from Abadan.

Upon hearing her cry, the Revolutionary Guards attacked her and brutally beat her. The next morning, 349 of the 350 inmates in this ward were hanged.

This is how the gem of honesty and sacrifice came into being, was enriched, and turned into a moral treasure for Iran's nation, for her freedom and her future.

So, we will repeat the poem written by Mahmoud Hassani, from Shahrood. As he was passing through the Death Tunnel of Evin Prison along with 60 of his Mojahed brothers, he whispered:

When in the dark of night, you see a bright meteor in the sky,
Do not forget the blazing flames that were extinguished in the cold nights of Evin,
So that a star would rise at dawn.

A blood-drenched encounter between the Middle Ages and future generations

The massacre of the PMOI and other combatant political prisoners was a blood-drenched encounter between the Middle Ages and future generations, the generations that created the 1979 revolution, who represented a nation committed to having a society based on freedom and equality. But that generation

PERPETRATORS MUST BE TRIED

30,000

ran into the monster of religious tyranny and the pillage and repression that ensued.

The massacre in 1988 was the horrifying scene of such a historic confrontation. But it was not the end. Despite its excruciating pain and agony, it was the beginning of a new confrontation which still continues and will ultimately write the fate of the Iranian nation with the word "freedom."

From this vantage point, one can see that the 1988 massacre is tied to Iran's freedom and future. It is entwined with the rights of human beings in Iran that are brutally violated, with the resistance for freedom and equality, with the betrayal of foreign proponents of appeasement, with the disgraceful cowardice of those who surrendered to the regime, and of course it is tied to the regime's overthrow. Because the day the Iranian people's Call-for-Justice movement compels these criminals to go public with the dossier of this atrocious crime, is the day when the rule of Velayat-e Faqih (absolute clerical rule) will end.

Time and again, we have heard in the witness testimonies that the imprisoned heroes hailed Massoud when they faced their torturers and executioners. They whispered to each other excerpts that they had memorized from his speeches, and during their visitations, they quietly sought updates and news about him through hand gestures and sign language.

In repeating this most crimson name of our time, they had and continue to have a message. Their message to succeeding generations and the youth who hear their unfinished stories is this: Follow the path and the ideal of Massoud Rajavi, a path that leads to a society devoid of all abuse and oppression, devoid of repression and tyranny, devoid of ignorance and deception; the path and ideal that is summarized in the sacred word, freedom.

Khomeini's intention for ordering the 1988 massacre was to uproot the Mojahedin

As Khomeini wrote in his religious decree (fatwa), his intention for ordering the 1988 massacre was to uproot and obliterate the Mojahedin. To this end, he deployed his killing machine in several arenas:

The most intense killings of the 1988 massacre began in Evin and Gohardasht prisons and were specifically aimed at PMOI members. Khomeini's heir at the time, Hossein Ali Montazeri, described the killings in these two prisons as a "slaughter… which has not taken place anywhere else in the world."

> **Khomeini said the regime's judges must not waste any time sending the prisoners' files to provincial capitals, and that they must have the PMOI members executed in whatever prison they were imprisoned.**

On August 25, 1988, the President of the National Council of Resistance of Iran, Massoud Rajavi, sent a telegram to UN Secretary General Javeir Pres de Cuellar, in which he said, "On August 14, 15, and 16 alone, 860 corpses belonging to the executed political prisoners were transferred from Evin Prison in Tehran to the Behesht-e Zahra Cemetery."

Mrs. Maryam Rajavi and mother of Rezaii martiers

Another important part of the massacre was the widespread killings which took place in prisons located in provincial capitals and other cities based on a second edict from Khomeini. In that edict, Khomeini said the regime's judges must not waste any time sending the prisoners' files to provincial capitals, and that they must have the PMOI members executed in whatever prison they were imprisoned.

The latest list of victims compiled by the PMOI/MEK indicates that the 1988 massacre took place in at least 110 cities.

In the exhibition (at Ashraf 3) which depicts the Iranian people's historical fight against the mullahs' religious tyranny, there is a remarkable scene. The maps of Iran's provinces, one by one, show that all of them without any exceptions, were scenes of countless executions both in the 1988 massacre and also during the unremitting executions which took place in the 1980s and afterwards.

That is, the people of Iran belonging to all ethnic groups or religions, from all cities or provinces, have paid the heaviest price and are united for the regime's overthrow and achieving freedom.

> **The massacre in 1988 was the horrifying scene of such a historic confrontation. But it was not the end. Despite its excruciating pain and agony, it was the beginning of a new confrontation which still continues and will ultimately write the fate of the Iranian nation with the word "freedom."**

It is not an accident that these cities and provinces are still hotbeds of constant uprisings and protests, and that these cities rise up one after the other in protest.

Our society has a burning fire in its heart, leaving Khamenei at an impasse. So, the regime's overthrow is the definite and certain fate for the mullahs.

Arrest and execution of former prisoners or supporters of the PMOI/MEK

Another important development taking place outside the prisons but parallel to the massacres inside was the widespread arrests of former prisoners or supporters of the PMOI/MEK, and their subsequent executions.

In the same month when the massacre started, the NCRI President wrote in a telegram to the UN Secretary General, revealing that simultaneous with the mass executions of political prisoners, an extensive wave of political arrests had been launched in various Iranian cities which included the arrests of over 10,000 persons.

Subsequently, Prof. Kazem Rajavi, the great martyr for the cause of human rights in Iran --who was also the NCRI's representative at the formal session of the UN Commission investigating political disappearances at the United Nations Palace in Geneva—said in a speech, "In the midst of accepting

the UN Security Council resolution (for the ceasefire of the Iran-Iraq war), the Khomeini regime has directed its wrath towards supporters of the Iranian Resistance inside Iran. Since the day of the announcement of the ceasefire, hundreds of persons from various cities have been abducted every day, and secretly sent before firing squads or incarcerated in prisons."

And yet another part of this massacre was the emergency trials of supporters of the Mojahedin in western Iran.

On July 24, 1988, Khomeini issued a secret edict to hold emergency trials under the pretext of "investigating war crimes." He appointed mullah Ali Razini as the head of this court. The complete text of this secret edict was exposed three months later by the Iranian Resistance.

In the following days, however, the court rapidly changed its course and took aim at supporters of the Mojahedin in western Iran. The victims were residents of western regions of Iran who had supported the Mojahedin as well as young men and women from other provinces who had gone to western regions to aid the Mojahedin.

On August 17, 1988, the NCRI President sent another telegram to the UN and leaders of the five permanent members of the Security Council warning against widespread executions of individuals who had not been involved in the battles of the National Liberation Army, and were being executed merely for supporting the PMOI/MEK.

Silence and giving impunity to the ruling murderers by the West in favor of the policy of appeasement

In outlining these incidents, I would like to recall that the Iranian Resistance actively made revelations regarding the 1988 massacre at the international level since the very first weeks, urging reaction by the world and especially western governments. However, they maintained their silence because they had just initiated their policy of appeasement.

In fact, one of the most harmful consequences of the policy of appeasement was providing impunity to the ruling murderers, whose crimes started in the early 1980s, reached new heights during the 1988 massacre and have continued to this day.

Giving impunity to the clerical regime's leaders provided them the opportunity to deny this crime according to an organized plan, just as they carried out the massacre of prisoners and the detainees, in accordance with a well-planned scheme.

Since 1988, the Iranian regime has taken numerous measures to eliminate traces of the mass graves belonging to the victims of the 1988 massacre all across Iran. They have built new buildings and roads on these grave yards, or have bulldozed them and turned them into new cemeteries. They have arrested and tortured families who sought to find the graves of their loved ones.

A considerable amount of information, even pictures

and images of such destructions, have been published. The international community, however, has not reacted, instead choosing to maintain its silence.

The regime ruling Iran has evaded publishing the information and details of the massacre of political prisoners, but has remained immune from international accountability.

They have refused to provide families the addresses of the graves of those executed. They have destroyed the mass graves, but have remained immune from any form of accountability.

The highest officials in charge of this crime and members of the Death Committees are among the senior officials presently running this regime, including the regime's Chief Justice and head of the Judiciary, the Head of the Supreme Court and the so-called Justice Minister. All of them, however, are immune.

A number of them, including the mullahs' supreme leader Ali Khamenei, defend the 1988 massacre. They even say that they are proud of it. And still, they enjoy impunity.

As Amnesty International pointed out in its report on the 1988 massacre last December, Iran faced an impunity crisis, and the continuity of crimes in Iran are directly related to the impunity the Iranian regime officials enjoy.

Granting impunity to the regime's leaders and turning a blind eye to their crimes is the very reason they have become emboldened in exporting terrorism and in warmongering.

> **"As Amnesty International pointed out in its report on the 1988 massacre last December, Iran faced an impunity crisis, and the continuity of crimes in Iran are directly related to the impunity the Iranian regime officials enjoy."**

Time to end three decades of impunity of regime's leaders

The time has come for the international community to end three decades of impunity for the clerical regime leaders in Iran and to hold them accountable for their crimes.

The time has come for referring the dossier of human rights violations in Iran, particularly the executions of the 1980s and the 1988 massacre, to the UN Security Council.

The time has come for Khamenei and his accomplices to face justice for committing crimes against humanity.

The time has come for the United Nations to launch an international fact-finding mission into the 1988 massacre in Iran.

“The time has come for referring the dossier of human rights violations in Iran, particularly the executions of the 1980s and the 1988 massacre, to the UN Security Council.”

And the time has come for the world to recognize the right of the people of Iran to resistance and struggle to overthrow the mullahs' religious fascism.

I urge the international community, the UN Security Council, the UN Human Rights Council and its member states, as well as other relevant United Nation agencies, the European Union, and all advocates of human rights and justice, to rise up and to end the impunity of those responsible for the 1988 massacre.

How could the world tolerate sitting in the United Nations side by side with those directly involved in the massacre of tens of thousands of prisoners? How could they negotiate and engage in commerce with them? This is a travesty for human rights. This is providing space for extremism and fundamentalism. This is trampling upon justice and democracy, not only in Iran but throughout the Middle East and all around the world. The massacre of political prisoners in Iran has been the worst massacre of prisoners since the Second World War.

The Call-for-Justice movement for the victims of the 1988 massacre is the movement of the oppressed

I call on all compatriots in Iran and abroad to help advance and expand the Call-for-Justice movement for the victims of the 1988 massacre, to any extent and in any form. This is the movement of the oppressed. This is the movement of those who are suppressed. This is the movement of the bereaved. Anyone who has experienced any number of days in prison and captivity, anyone who has been flogged, and any woman who is outraged or humiliated, is a member of this movement. And anyone whose conscience is wounded by so many crimes, is a member of this movement.

One day, we raised the banner of peace vis-à-vis Khomeini's warmongering and belligerence, and insisted on it for so long that we managed to pour the poison chalice of ceasefire in the Iran-Iraq war down Khomeini's throat, thanks to the operations of the National Liberation Army.

We also rose up against the mullahs' ominous bomb-making program. And we persevered so long that we poured the poison chalice of the nuclear deal down Khamenei's throat.

Now, we have vowed to stand firm on this call for justice. We will persevere until we pour the poison chalice of human rights and the poison chalice of the 1988 massacre down the throat of this regime. Yes, 1,000 chalices of poison serving the cause of 1,000 Ashrafs to bring down the mullahs and to establish freedom.

The Call-for-Justice movement carries on. We will continue until all the details of this horrible crime are revealed, until the graves of all our sisters and brothers are found, until the regime of massacre is overthrown by the people of Iran, their resistance units and their great Army of Freedom.

We salute the martyrs

And we hail freedom

Maryam Rajavi's messages to Iranians participating in rallies in five major world capitals

In response to the call by the Iranian Resistance's leader Massoud Rajavi, freedom loving Iranians held extensive rallies in Brussels, Washington, D.C., Berlin, Stockholm, and London in solidarity with the Iranian people's uprisings and Resistance for regime change. They declared support for the resistance units inside Iran, the National Liberation Army and the democratic alternative, the National Council of Resistance of Iran.

The rallies and marches were held in Brussels on June 15, Washington, D.C. on June 21, Berlin on July 6, Stockholm on July 20, and London on July 27, 2019.

Iranians took to the streets of major capitals of the world to condemn flagrant violations of human rights in Iran, the Iranian regime's terrorism and warmongering in the region, and to convey the voice of the people of Iran and their Liberation Army to the world's public.

In her messages to these rallies, Maryam Rajavi commended her fellow Iranians who participated.

Maryam Rajavi:
We urge the EU to impose comprehensive sanctions on Iran's theocratic regime

Message to the rally of Iranians before EU headquarters in Brussels

June 15, 2019

01

Your gathering today symbolizes our national dignity and conscience

As we approach June 20, the anniversary of the onset of our historical resistance for freedom and popular sovereignty against the mullahs' absolute dictatorship, the Day of Martyrs and Political Prisoners, and the founding anniversary of the National Liberation Army of Iran, your gathering today fans the flames of hope and symbolizes our national dignity and conscience.

It flies the flag of our nation's proud steadfastness in the face of a vicious and reactionary regime. Your gathering today is the epitome of a glorious future towards which we are moving.

Freedom cannot be achieved unless you have a long line of selfless men and women firmly determined to persevere and resist for achieving freedom without having any personal interests or expecting any rewards for themselves.

Hail to the brave men and women of the resistance units and popular resistance councils who have formed this long line all across Iran. And hail to you who have extended this line to the heart of Europe in front of the European Union's headquarters in Brussels.

Desire of Iranian people, the overthrow of the regime in its entirety

Dear compatriots,

The decadent regime of the mullahs is surrounded by infuriated people fed up with the status quo, to the extent that just like the final days of the Shah's regime, Majlis deputies openly express their alarm during the parliamentary sessions, and one after the other warn against the regime's calamitous destiny.

> “Freedom cannot be achieved unless you have a long line of selfless men and women firmly determined to persevere and resist for achieving freedom”

They openly challenge the regime's president and dare him to eat like the rest of the people for just one month to see if he can tolerate such conditions.

Rouhani and his ministers also say that the situation of the regime has never been so dire over the past 40 years.

At the top, the white turbaned mullah (Rouhani) blames the black turbaned mullah (Khamenei) for flaws, demanding more

authority. But Khamenei's response was that they should prepare to convene a solid Hezbollahi government.

For the people of Iran, however, there is no difference between black turbans and white turbans. They want the overthrow of the entire regime and they cry out, "Our enemy is right here."

Now, if anyone claims to be able to change the behavior of the mullahs' religious fascist regime by offering economic and political incentives without budging on the human rights of the people of Iran and their right to sovereignty, we would happily welcome this option and encourage them to go ahead and change the regime's behavior as much as they can.

FREE
IRAN

Recognizing the Iranian people's right to Resistance

The polarization between the regime and anti-regime fronts is being highlighted more and more as we approach the end of the clerical regime. The regime's proponents and those who have interests in perpetuating its rule, encourage giving concessions and appeasing Iran's ruling murderers while projecting concern about the outbreak of a war.

As Massoud Rajavi says, those concerned about the fate of the Iranian regime keep warning against the outbreak of a war at any decisive juncture. "The worst likely mistake for the U.S. and international community with regards to the clerical regime is trying to avoid a war."

> "We demand that the regime's terrorist diplomat arrested in Belgium be prosecuted as soon as possible. This is the right of Iranian refugees to learn the details of the mullahs' terrorist"

He adds, "Four decades of experience prove that the worst mistake is budging and hesitating to hit the head of the serpent with a rock. Without this, i.e. overthrowing this regime, Iran could not be freed. And this is a duty solely on the shoulders of the Iranian people and their Resistance. Therefore, it is imperative to recognize the right of the people of Iran to resist against and overthrow the mullahs' regime."

The regime's solution to preserve its rule amidst such terminal crises has been to demonize the PMOI/MEK and the Iranian Resistance as their main existential threat, an effort which has led to terrorism.

By demonizing the Mojahedin, the regime seeks to arrange the scene in such a way that everyone would conclude that the clerical regime is better and is what the Iranian people deserve. So, they would be better off giving up resistance and continue their life in misery.

Call to the European Union

The terrorist operations in Europe, the attempted bombings in Albania and France, the arrests of the Iranian regime's mercenaries and its terrorist diplomat Assadollah Assadi, and the expulsions of four of the regime's terrorist diplomats over the past year, all verified the Iranian Resistance's repeated disclosures that the Iranian regime's embassies in Europe are all centers for planning and carrying out the regime's criminal plots.

> "The ruling regime cannot withstand our nation's resistance and uprisings and their great Army of Freedom."

#TeamJunckerEU
Europese
Commissie

UN IRAN
LIBRE
MARYAM
RADJAVI

> **The regime's leaders must face justice in an international tribunal and account for their crimes against the people of Iran and particularly the massacre of political prisoners in 1988.**

We demand that the regime's terrorist diplomat arrested in Belgium be prosecuted as soon as possible. It is the right of Iranian refugees to learn the details of the mullahs' terrorist plots in foreign countries. And this is the requisite to any effort to prevent similar incidents in the future.

> **We call on the European Union to impose comprehensive sanctions on the theocratic regime ruling Iran, and to designate the mullahs' Revolutionary Guard Corps (IRGC) and their**

We call on the European Union to impose comprehensive sanctions on the theocratic regime ruling Iran, and to designate the mullahs' Islamic Revolutionary Guard Corps (IRGC) and their Ministry of Intelligence (MOIS) as terrorist entities. The regime's mercenaries must be tried, punished and expelled.

The regime's leaders must face justice in an international tribunal and be held to account for their crimes against the people of Iran and particularly the massacre of political prisoners in 1988.

Dear friends,

The sensitivity of the present juncture and the increasing weakening of the clerical regime place the burden of responsibility on the shoulders of each and every one of us. Beyond a shadow of a doubt, the ruling regime cannot withstand our nation's resistance and uprisings and their great Army of Freedom.

Hail to freedom

Hail to all of you

Maryam Rajavi: The Iranian nation hears your anthems and your cries for freedom

Message to the Iranians' rally

in Washington, D.C.

June 21, 2019

02

What is the real question for US and European policies vis-a-vis the fascist religious regime ruling Iran?

Fellow citizens, freedom-loving Iranians, sympathizers and friends of the Iranian Resistance,

Rebels for Iran's freedom, who have travelled all the way from across the U.S., to come together today in Washington, D.C.

The Iranian nation hears your anthems and your cries for freedom.

Today, you are the voice of an oppressed nation whose assets have been robbed.

Greetings to you, to the elected representatives of the American people who are here, and to personalities and long-time friends and supporters of the Iranian people's Resistance for democracy and human rights. They have all come today to stand with you.

Congratulations on the anniversary of the resistance, June 20, the Day of Martyrs and Political Prisoners, and on the anniversary of the founding of the Army of Freedom; a movement that has unceasingly forged ahead in all theatres for four decades, relying on its own toil, struggle and sacrifice.

Sovereignty of the people vs. the mullahs' rule

To fend off the people's fury, for forty years, the murderous mullahs have pointed their fingers at the U.S. as the enemy. But we were not deceived. As Massoud Rajavi has said: "When we declared 'down with the reactionaries,' we stood by it. We have and will continue to declare that what we seek is the regime's overthrow, overthrow, overthrow."

Now, the people of Iran cry out in every street and alley that "our enemy is right here; the mullahs lie when they say America is the enemy."

Indeed, this is a regime whose Constitution has formally replaced people's sovereignty and universal suffrage with the rule of the mullahs.

The medieval mullahs tell the Resistance's freedom fighters and Army of Freedom:

❍ Give up and surrender, otherwise you are infidels and pagans who wage war on God. You are agents of the Global Arrogance; you are a sect and you do not have a place or any base of support among the people in Iran.

❍ Do not resist, otherwise you are terrorists. Otherwise, you are going to be deluged by fake allegations.

Yes, the disgraceful demonization campaign against the Iranian Resistance in the pro-appeasement media seeks to perpetuate the narrative that the people of Iran are better off with the theocratic rule of the mullahs; There is no alternative, and don't even think or talk about it.

Their conclusion is:

❍ The religious fascism must be appeased and there are no

#FreeIran
#FreeIran
March in Solidarity with the Uprising
and the Iranian Resistance for Regime Cha

other options.

- Now, if the U.S. administration does not appease the mullahs' tyranny, it would be a warmonger.
- If the U.S. obstructs the Iranian regime's path toward nuclear weapons, it would be a warmonger.

"When the mullahs pay no price for their conducts, they become more emboldened and go even further. Firing of rockets in Mosul and Basra and the missile attack on the U.S. drone are clear examples."

The absurd comments made by the mullahs and their Foreign Minister about the so-called "B Team" in the United States was a bid to hide their own "bomb" team: From developing a nuclear bomb to bombings in Albania and France, to bombings and planting of mines on oil tankers in the Persian Gulf, to the explosions, drones and missile attacks on Saudi Arabia and targeting of the U.S. Embassy in Baghdad.

When the mullahs pay no price for their conducts, they become more emboldened and go even further. Firing of rockets in Mosul and Basra and the missile attack on the U.S. drone are clear examples.

Indeed, who is the belligerent party? Who launched consecutive rocket and missile attacks at camps Ashraf and Liberty?

Before the terrorist designation of the Islamic Revolutionary

"What is the real question before us, our people and our resistance? To surrender or to fight for liberation.

Consider the American Declaration of Independence. The question before George Washington, Thomas Jefferson, Benjamin Franklin and their comrades and supporters was the same. And, similarly, our answer is the same: To resist and fight until victory."

Guard Corps (IRGC) and the imposition of sanctions, and before the U.S. pulled out of the nuclear deal, the mullahs had no qualms about claiming that Syria was Iran's 35th province. They did not hesitate to say that Iraq was their "center and capital" and even that "its geography is inseparable from Iran's."

The current IRGC commander-in-chief once explicitly said: "The geography of our revolution has extended to northern Africa." He then went on to warn that "it was the flames of the Islamic Revolution that flared" in 1983 in Lebanon, "where a courageous move by a young Muslim buried 260 U.S. marines under the rubble in Beirut, east of the Mediterranean Sea."

Yes, the people of Iran who have been inundated by floods, destitution and various calamities, are crying out, "Let go of Syria and think about us instead." But the regime's meddling and crimes in Iraq, Syria, Yemen, Lebanon and Afghanistan have so far brought them no serious consequences.

Appeasement or decisiveness?

Indeed, what is the real question at the core of the U.S. and European policy vis-a-vis the religious fascist regime ruling Iran: appeasement or decisiveness?

The closer we get to the end of this regime, the contradiction and polarization between the regime and regime opponents become more conspicuous.

For the past forty years, the regime has persistently waged wars against the people of Iran and the world. Still, regime apologists and those who benefit from its continued rule feign concern for war. They use this as a pretext to dissuade the world from adopting any form of decisiveness, and instead urge appeasement of the ruling murderers in Iran.

The main victims, however, are the people of Iran. The experience of the past 40 years has demonstrated that the mullahs' theocratic regime is incapable of any reform or change of behavior. Indeed, as a (Persian) saying goes, "a viper will never give birth to a dove."

Khamenei says that change in the regime's behavior is tantamount to regime change.

Therefore, what is the real question before us, our people and our resistance? To surrender or to fight for liberation.

Consider the American Declaration of Independence. The question before George Washington, Thomas Jefferson, Benjamin Franklin and their comrades and supporters was the same. And, similarly, our answer is the same: To resist and fight until victory.

> **"Now, the people of Iran cry out in every street and alley that "our enemy is right here; the mullahs lie when they say America is the enemy.""**

The people of Iran desire freedom and human rights

Hail to the brave women and men who have swelled the ranks in their quest for freedom in the form of resistance units and popular resistance councils, and you should be proud to have extended these ranks to the U.S. capital.

Three months ago, for the first time in the past 70 years, the President of the United States in his Nowruz (Persian New Year) message to the people of Iran attested to the fact that:

> "The disgraceful demonization campaign against the Iranian Resistance in the pro-appeasement media seeks to perpetuate the narrative that the people of Iran are better off with the theocratic rule of the mullahs; there is no alternative, and don't even think or talk about it."

"The Iranian people desire to reclaim their country's proud history, expressive culture, and rightful place on the world stage. They deserve a government that is accountable to them and that treats them with dignity and respect."

He emphasized: "We pledge never to turn a deaf ear to the

calls of the Iranian people for freedom, and we will never forget their ongoing struggle for human rights."

Yes, we do not want anything more than freedom and human rights, which will of course also open the way for us toward development and justice.

This will ensue peace and security in Iran and the Middle East; an Iran free of religious fascism, a non-nuclear Iran and an Iran without terrorism and belligerence.

Freedom will prevail over the Shah and the mullahs

> "It is right at this point that it becomes clear that the religious dictatorship is a paper tiger when it comes to facing off with the Iranian Resistance. And its fate is no different from the fate of the Shah's dictatorship. This is the verdict of history and the yearning of the people of Iran."

As Massoud Rajavi has said, this outcome will "offer peace, security, democracy, human rights, stability, rebuilding, friendship, and a non-nuclear Iran that seeks economic cooperation and development in this part of the world, and a country that will respect international laws and conventions."

This is why, above and beyond anything else, the mullahs are most fearful of change at the hands of the Iranian people, the Iranian Resistance and the People's Mojahedin Organization of Iran (PMOI/MEK).

It is right at this point that it becomes clear that the religious dictatorship is a paper tiger when it comes to facing off with the Iranian Resistance. And its fate is no different from the fate of the Shah's dictatorship. This is the verdict of history and the yearning of the people of Iran.

Yes, freedom will prevail over the Shah and the Sheikh (mullahs).

My fellow citizens,

Dear friends who have defied religious dictatorship and fascism,

The regime is getting weaker by the day, and with every passing day it gets a step closer to its downfall.

Consequently, all of us bear heavier responsibilities.

This is the time for us to be on alert.

Without a doubt, the faltering mullahs' dictatorship cannot withstand our nation's resistance, uprisings, and the great Army of Freedom.

Hail to freedom

Hail to all of you

Maryam Rajavi: We call on all countries to join the international front against religious fascism

Message to the rally of Iranians in Berlin

July 6, 2019

03

Stop the policy of giving concessions to the religious dictatorship

Dear compatriots,

Your presence here, in this third demonstration following the major gatherings and rallies of our friends and compatriots in Brussels and Washington, D.C., has a clear message.

Addressing our country, those who have risen up, workers, teachers, and other people who are fed up with the regime, you say, advance ahead as quickly as you can because the mullahs are stuck in the trap of their downfall.

In this grand demonstration, your message and the message of the people of Iran to the world and particularly to Europe is this: Stop the policy of giving concessions to the religious dictatorship.

The policy of protecting the mullahs against being overthrown and the policy of feeding the turbaned mullahs do not solve any problems for this regime.

> “Why have Germany and the European Union not declared the Revolutionary Guard Corps (IRGC) a terrorist entity?”

Isn't 40 years enough for espousing the mirage of reform and the myth of moderation in the clerical regime?

Where did thirty years of constructive dialogue, critical dialogue and dialogues about all sorts of incentives end up?

Didn't you see how the uprisings and the protest movement in Iran pushed the regime to its terminal phase?

Didn't the mullahs' espionage and terrorist operations in Europe and on the soil of Germany toll the knell for policy change?

Were the regime's belligerence, missile attacks, recent attacks on oil tankers and the downing of the American drone not enough to consider revising this policy?

Rouhani has been the focal point of Europe's hope for moderation from within the regime. Now, he boasts about kissing the hands of the Revolutionary Guards for their missile attacks. Didn't this remove the most significant excuse for getting along with the mullahs' religious fascism?

Isn't 40 years enough for espousing the mirage of reform and the myth of moderation and reform in the clerical regime?

Everyone remembers that a decade ago, when the regime's former president howled that the Holocaust is not true, the German Chancellor reacted by saying, "In 1933, too, Nazi mottos were projected as insignificant remarks. But Germany has learned from its history and is obliged to confront what is in the making."

Let me ask this: Did the history of Germany and other European nations not teach the world what a heavy and bloody price humanity has to pay for appeasement of fascism?

Exactly one year ago, Germany arrested a so-called diplomat of the regime who had personally handed explosives to two terrorists to use against the Resistance's grand gathering in Paris.

Before and after that, the German Police arrested a dozen mercenaries and terrorists over three years, who had ties with the terrorist Quds Force and the Ministry of Intelligence. A number of them were tried and imprisoned by the German Judiciary.

"Did the history of Germany and other European nations not teach the world what a heavy and bloody price humanity has to pay for appeasement of fascism?"

The question is why don't such significant incidents bring about any change in Germany's policy towards the Iranian regime?

The mullahs shamelessly speak of resorting to uranium enrichment and preparing for a nuclear bomb every day. Salehi, head of the regime's Atomic Energy Organization, admitted that the regime had deceived European countries regarding the nuclear site in Arak.

Indeed, if the mullahs were not so sure of their relations with Europe, how could they be so insolent?

From expanding their ballistic missiles program in violation of the UNSC resolution 2231, to dispatching forces to Syria in violation of the UNSC resolution 2254, and stepping up their criminal war in that country, the religious fascism in Iran is indeed the greatest threat to peace in the world today.

The mullahs' regime has declared war on the peoples of Iran and the region for the past 40 years. So, every concession to them under any pretext has only one outcome: Increasing the likelihood of a disastrous war by the mullahs.

Every one Euro of trade with the mullahs, is equal to one Euro of fuel for Khamenei's machine to clamp down on the people of Iran and trigger a war in the region. Speaking of peace in the region is a hollow motto if it is not accompanied by sanctions on Khamenei and the Revolutionary Guards.

But let me stress: Regime change is the task of the Iranian people and their Resistance. It is the job of the Army of Freedom and no one else.

As Massoud Rajavi has told young Iranian protestors: The people of Iran have the last say through their resistance units and the Liberation Army.

Do not help the mullahs remain in power

What we have urged is that western governments do not help the mullahs remain in power. Wasn't the terrorist designation of the PMOI/MEK and suppression of the Mojahedin and Iranian Resistance in European countries, a disgraceful deal and the best assistance to the mullahs?

What about leaving out the violations of human rights in

IRAN

IRAN with Maryam

Iran from the nuclear agreement? What about leaving the path open for the regime's expansion of its nuclear facilities, some of whose equipment and technology are procured from your markets?

What about the sale of tools used for suppression, eavesdropping and espionage to the notorious Ministry of Intelligence and the Revolutionary Guard Corps? And what about providing forums for the regime's demonization efforts by publishing volumes of fake news against the Mojahedin in the pro-appeasement media?

Yes, all of these are assisting the mullahs.

Why is it that the Iranian Embassy is not shut down?

Germany's Department of Protection of the Constitution acknowledges every year, including just a few days ago, that the Iranian Embassy is engaged in espionage against their opponents, particularly against the Mojahedin (PMOI/MEK) and the National Council of Resistance of Iran (NCRI). So, why is it that this embassy is not shut down?

The German Judiciary ruled that the mullahs' supreme leader, the regime's president, foreign minister and Ministry of Intelligence made the decision and ordered the terrorist assassinations in Mykonos Restaurant in Berlin. So, why is Khamenei not on the terror list of Germany and Europe, and why isn't he sanctioned by them?

The Government of Germany has also officially confirmed that the Iranian regime had a role in the attacks on oil tankers and has emphasized the regime's destructive role in the region. So, why have Germany and the European Union not declared the Revolutionary Guard Corps (IRGC) a terrorist entity?

I'd like to reiterate that the prosecution, punishment and expulsion of the mercenaries of the Iranian Intelligence Ministry and the Revolutionary Guard Corps, as well as the EU's declaration of April 29, 1997 must be implemented and enforced.

> **"The international community and specifically the European Union must recognize the right of the people of Iran for resistance to overthrow the mullahs' regime and establish a democratic government and the sovereignty of the people of Iran."**

The declaration, which was issued simultaneously with the court ruling on the case of Mykonos Restaurant, stresses that EU relations with the Iranian regime must be contingent and conditioned on the regime officials' respect for the standards of international law and its abstention from terrorist activities.

It also called for refusing visas to the agents of the Iranian regime's intelligence and security agencies and focusing on the expulsion of the regime's intelligence agents from EU member states.

It is imperative and urgent for Iranians and their security that the articles of the April 29, 1997 declaration be executed.

As for human rights, please allow me to particularly ask Mrs. Merkel to lead a special initiative on the European level against the clerical regime's violations of human rights to stop among others the persecution, execution and murder of prisoners under torture, and to form an international delegation to visit Iranian prisons and political prisoners.

Call on international community

On behalf of the Iranian people's Resistance, I would like to reiterate that:

The international community and specifically the European Union must recognize the right of the people of Iran for resistance to overthrow the mullahs' regime and to establish a democratic government and the sovereignty of the people of Iran.

The dossier of human rights abuses and massacre of political prisoners in Iran must be referred to the UN Security Council.

The United Nations' Security Council must declare that the clerical regime in Iran is a threat to global peace and security.

We also call on all countries to join the international front against the religious fascism.

And finally, I would like to extend my warmest gratitude to the German dignitaries and members of parliament, especially the members of the German Committee in Solidarity with a Free Iran. The support and assistance of these honorable women and men are a golden page in the history of relations between the nations of Germany and Iran.

IRAN

Stop Mullahs' regime Terrorism in Europe & Prosecute its Agents
Stoppt den Mullah-Terror in Europa & klagt seine Agenten an

I would like to honor the memory of our dear Ingrid Holzhüter who supported the Mojahedin and residents of Ashraf until her last day.

I would like to remember Gaok, the German comrade of Mirza Kuchek Khan, who remained loyal to him to the last moment of his life and died with him, thus becoming the historic symbol of friendship between our two nations.

Yes, with a nation determined to overthrow the mullahs' regime, with your passion and love of freedom, and with the resolve of resistance units and the battle waged by the Army of Freedom, Iran will be free.

> **"What we have urged is that western governments do not help the mullahs remain in power."**

Time for a FREE IRAN
with Maryam RAJAVI

IRAN
with
Maryam
STOP
Executions
in
IRAN

Maryam Rajavi: Nordic countries must recognize the right of Iranian people for resistance to overthrow the mullahs' regime

Message to the Iranians' rally in Stockholm

July 20, 2019

04

Our salutes to Mossadeq and to the martyrs of the uprising on July 21, 1952

Fellow Iranians,

Tomorrow is July 21, the 67th anniversary of our people's national uprising where people chanted, "We give our lives to bring back Mossadeq." He embodied the Iranian people's sovereignty in the face of the monarchic dictatorship and the reactionary mullahs.

It is also the 38th anniversary of the foundation of the National Council of Resistance of Iran, announced by Massoud Rajavi on July 21, 1981, in Tehran.

Indeed, Massoud has safeguarded Mossadeq's name and memory in Iran's contemporary history, and followed and improved his path since the time he was in torture chambers, during his trial and up until today.

This has been especially valuable at a time when Khomeini expressed gratitude for what he described as "the slapping of Mossadeq" by the reactionary mullahs and colonialists. He openly admitted that he could not tolerate meetings held in honor of Mossadeq, saying, "If someone nationalized the oil, it is no reason for people to set aside Islam to defend him."

Really, what was the message of Mossadeq?

On Reza Khan's despotism and his coup d'etat, Mossadeq said, "Is it possible to make a revolution and lead people in the right direction with the help of a Cossack brigade taking orders from foreigners? Could anyone become a revolutionary or claim reforms by issuing a hollow statement? Which insightful person is deceived by such talks?"

In another place, he added, "Do not turn in the standard-bearers of freedom to the executioners who serve reactionary fundamentalism."

Our salutes to Mossadeq, to the martyrs of the uprising on July 21, 1952, and their successors in history.

And this is a path that will be paved in the resistance for freedom until final victory and achieving a free Iran; a prospect that is becoming brighter every day.

The myth of moderation of this regime, no longer deceives anyone

By displaying your remarkable determination and resolve, and the wide scope and dynamism of this movement which extends from resistance units in cities across Iran to the grand gatherings and rallies in various countries of the world, you have demonstrated the Iranian nation's iron will for the overthrow of the mullah's dictatorship.

The time has come for putting an end to the appeasement of the religious fascism in Iran. There are no more excuses for overlooking the enemy of the people of Iran.

No longer can anyone claim that the regime has no alternative, and that this regime is better for the people of Iran.

I specifically urge the governments of Sweden, Norway, Denmark and Finland to pressure the Iranian regime to open its prisons to visits by an international fact-finding mission.

Maryam Rajavi

No longer can anyone set their sights for 8 years on Rafsanjani's moderation, and 8 years on reforms by Khatami, and another 8 years on moderation of Rouhani who has repeatedly declared that he kisses the hands of Khamenei and his Revolutionary Guard Corps.

Then you wake up late and see that the clerical regime is only one year away from the nuclear bomb, has gained strongholds in Iraq, Syria and Yemen and has a missile program which it says is non-negotiable.

Indeed, has the clerical regime left any room to hope for the slightest accountability for human rights, for freedom of speech, for justice, for gender equality, or for the rights and autonomy of ethnic groups and religious minorities?

The myth of moderation of this regime, illusions about any likely reforms in it, and constructive and critical dialogue with it, no longer deceive anyone. The Iranian Resistance has paid the heaviest price to prove that such claims are hollow.

> No longer can anyone set their sights for 8 years on Rafsanjani's moderation, and 8 years on reforms by Khatami, and another 8 years on moderation of Rouhani who has repeatedly declared that he kisses the hands of Khamenei and his Revolutionary Guard Corps.

One must always fight on and on

Unjust designations of the PMOI and the Iranian Resistance no longer have any impact.

The roaring blood of the martyrs and the Iranian people's steadfastness and uprisings have driven the Velayat-e Faqih (absolute clerical rule) regime to the end of the line. It has brought about a disgraceful defeat for the policy of appeasement of the mullahs' evil rule.

Conscientious human beings from across Europe and

> **Gunnar Sønsteby used to say, "I know that when someone fights for freedom, he/she is called terrorist. Just as German fascists called me and my friends terrorists; they followed us and wanted to execute us."**

Scandinavia have always recalled the bitter experience of appeasing fascism, namely the Nazi invaders, in confronting the religious fascism in Iran.

At this point, I would like to salute Gunnar Sønsteby, Norway's resistance fighter and war hero. He supported the Mojahedin of Ashraf and described the determined and steadfast men and women of Ashraf as living examples of a legendary resistance.

He used to tell us, "To achieve democracy and freedom, one must always fight on and on and on." He used to say, "I know that when someone fights for freedom, he/she is called terrorist. Just as German fascists called me and my friends terrorists; they

blidka

followed us and wanted to execute us."

So, we have always kept in mind Gunnar's brilliant advice that "one must always fight on and on."

We should not let the dignity of resistance for freedom which has created heroes like Gunnar be tarnished with commercial and trade interests.

Europe should side with the desires of Iran's nation

The people of Iran expect Europe, which has suffered tremendously in the past century from the reign of Hitler's fascism, to understand and feel the suffering of Iranian people today. Europe should side with the desires of Iran's nation.

Now that Finland is president of the European Union, it must focus EU sanctions on the regime's main levers of suppressions of freedom, and against its terrorism and suppression, namely Khamenei's office, the Revolutionary Guard Corps (IRGC) and the Ministry of Intelligence and Security (MOIS).

“The people of Iran expect Europe which has suffered tremendously in the past century from the reign of Hitler's fascism, to understand and feel the suffering of Iranian people today. Europe should side with the desires of Iran's nation.”

The regime's mercenaries must be tried, punished and expelled.

I specifically urge the governments of Sweden, Norway, Denmark and Finland to pressure the Iranian regime to open its prisons to visits by an international fact-finding mission.

Nordic countries, all of Europe, and the world must recognize the right of the people of Iran for resistance to overthrow the clerical regime and to establish democracy and popular sovereignty.

Yes, freedom will prevail,
Iran will be free,
With your support, a free Iran is on its way,
Hail to you all.

Maryam Rajavi: We urge Britain and Europe to stand on the side of the people of Iran for regime change

Message to the Iranians' rally in London

July 27, 2019

05

Regime change and regime change...

Fellow countrymen and women,

Your demonstration today in London marks the peak of a series of Free Iran rallies that have taken place over the past one-and-a-half months in Brussels, Washington, D.C., Berlin, and Stockholm.

It is also an extension of the Iranian Resistance's 5-day annual gatherings, two weeks ago, at Ashraf 3.

The clerical regime has again unleashed another barrage of fake and misleading news against the Iranian Resistance through a fake twitter account presumably belonging to a French Consul General. The Foreign Ministry of France issued an official statement denying the news, and Twitter also shut down the regime's fake account.

The mullahs' regime has reiterated time and again that they do not have a red line and they tolerate anything against the regime, even against Khamenei. However, just as it was the case during the massacre of political prisoners in 1988, the most forbidden name and the red line is the name of the PMOI/MEK.

This is the identity, path and tradition which terrifies the religious dictatorship even inside the regime's jails and torture chambers. Khomeini issued a fatwa ordering the massacre of anyone who remained loyal to the name and ideals of the PMOI. But the victims cried out Massoud Rajavi's name even at the gallows.

Hossein Ali Montazeri, Khomeini's designated heir at the time, said the PMOI cannot be eliminated through killings, but would rather spread wider.

Today, we see that the PMOI has expanded in Iran through the growth of resistance units and 1,000 Ashrafs.

The message of the people of Iran and supporters of Ashraf is the same everywhere: freedom and a free Iran. The mullahs must go. Regime change and regime change… And we do not get tired of repeating and insisting on these calls. We will cry out and repeat them again and again until the day they are realized. And of course, they would be certainly realized with your support.

Why and for what reason? As Massoud Rajavi has said, because of remaining loyal to our pledges and making endless sacrifices in Iran's history.

A glance over the list of execution victims, particularly the list of the victims of the 1988 massacre, reveals the truth of this statement.

Our people, our Resistance and the Mojahedin of Ashraf, have proven that they are prepared and ready to pay the price of freedom.

Let us take a look at the events which took place years ago on this day and on upcoming days, and the price paid for each of them.

The attack on Ashraf on July 28 and 29, 2009, simultaneous with the uprisings in Iran, where 13 Ashraf residents were killed and more than 500 wounded.

And the great patriotic epical operation in 1988 called Eternal Light.

We salute and pay tribute to the martyrs, the heroes and heroines, and the freedom fighters of the National Liberation Army.

Free Iran

Peace and freedom can only be earned through fighting the mullahs' dictatorship

When Iran was burning in the fire of Khomeini's unpatriotic war, the Army of Peace and Freedom rose up and poured the poison chalice of the ceasefire down Khomeini's throat. The price was some 2,000 martyrs from among the most valiant children of Iran who gave their lives in the battles of the Liberation Army. This is something that we are proud of. This is in addition to the Iranian Resistance's incessant revelations about the mullahs' bomb-making program and confronting their warmongering in the region.

Our Resistance has proven that peace and freedom can only be earned through fighting the mullahs' religious dictatorship. This is in diametric opposition to the proponents of appeasement who defend the regime under the guise of peace.

Recently, the mullahs welcomed publication of a book by Jack Straw, one of the proponents of the policy of appeasement. He paints firmness against the mullahs' religious fascism as a prelude to full-fledged war.

It is easy to guess that if it was the time of Hitler, how far he would go, as Winston Churchill said, to feed the crocodile.

It is not a coincidence that he was among the sponsors of the terrorist designation of the PMOI as well as their bombing and slaughter in 2003. Khatami and Kharrazi said that he was the man who said it was acceptable to demand the extradition

همبستگی با مقاومت ایران و قیام مردم
Solidarity with the Iranian Resistance & Iran Uprising

of PMOI members and hanging of at least 20 of their leaders. According to the Daily Telegraph, to curry favor with the mullahs, he had the list of the 12 Shiite Imams in his pocket when he visited Tehran. And when the name of the Prophet of Islam was mentioned anywhere, he whispered Muslim prayers.

These gentlemen's hollow calls for peace are tantamount to safeguarding the regime against the Iranian people's desire and against human rights.

Genuine calls for peace, however, can be realized only by peace and human rights. Its prerequisite is the overthrow of the ogre of war and oppression, the Velayat-e faqih (absolute clerical rule) dictatorship.

Indeed, are the mullahs' and IRGC's attacks on shipping in the Persian Gulf, which threaten regional and international security, in any way related to the policy of appeasement, the clampdown

> "The message of the people of Iran and supporters of Ashraf is the same everywhere: freedom and a free Iran. The mullahs must go."

on the PMOI, and overlooking the violations of human rights in Iran in the nuclear deal? Didn't concessions to the mullahs at the expense of the Iranian people and Resistance further embolden the mullahs?

How did the proscription of the PMOI, disarming the Liberation Army, and bombardments of their bases in those years, with UK's assistance, change the balance of power on the ground and in whose interest? Did they benefit peace and security or worked against them? Indeed, has the clerical regime given

FREE
IRAN
WITH
MARYAM
RAJAVI

up on its hostage taking of European and American citizens and nationals?

Why has the regime increased the level of uranium enrichment and why has it added to the range of its ballistic missiles?

Who benefits, and to what end, from the demonization of the PMOI and the Iranian Resistance?

Indeed, what happened to the moderate and reformed mullahs you encouraged and advocated for during four decades? What happened to so much propaganda and investments on charlatans such as Mohammmad Khatami? Didn't the people of Iran put an end to the political theatrics of fundamentalists vs. reformists through their uprisings?

Why do some people in Britain continue to subscribe to and

> **"Our Resistance has proven that peace and freedom can only be earned through fighting the mullahs' religious dictatorship. This is in diametric opposition to the proponents of appeasement who defend the regime under the guise of peace."**

relay the fake news and propaganda of the religious fascism in Iran?

Isn't it shameful to let mullah Khatami brazenly claim in the Guardian that he had spent all his life on dialogue among nations and civilizations, and on peace, democracy and human rights? This impostor mullah ordered the Iranian press not to mention even one word about the massacre of political prisoners (in 1988). He also gave free rein to the IRGC to do whatever they wanted to the students involved in the 1999 uprising and advised them to wear plain clothes.

Khatami who claims to be promoting civilization, culture and peace, is the one who zealously supported the regime's export of fundamentalism and was Khomeini's propaganda minister in the eight-year war when according to the regime's Education Minister 450,000 high school students were sent to the war front to clear mine fields.

Shame on the inhumane mullahs and their proponents. While waging war against the people of Iran they shamelessly call for a peace coalition, of course to preserve the regime's rule.

> **"The policy of giving manoeuvring room to the mullahs has been and continues to be totally disappointing and a disaster, This policy is not only against the people of Iran, but against regional and global peace and security"**

Six months ago, Mr. Tony Blair wrote in the Washington Post, "Hopes that this would lead the Tehran regime to moderate its behavior have proved misplaced." He wrote that the regime had intensified its malign policies around the region, in Syria, in Lebanon, in Iraq, in Yemen, in the Persian Gulf, and in the Palestinian territories…

And then he concluded that 40 years of disappointment should make us clear-eyed because the regime has turned into the "single biggest destabilizing force in the Middle East."

Yes, the policy of giving maneuvering room to the mullahs has been and continues to be totally disappointing and a disaster. This policy is not only against the people of Iran, but against regional and global peace and security.

The Iranian Resistance has paid the heaviest price and has always reiterated that the mullahs understand no other language except the language of force and firmness.

We urge Britain, Europe and all governments to halt giving concessions to the mullahs. Do not help them lessen the impact of sanctions. Stand up to them. Place the Islamic Revolutionary Guard Corps (IRGC) and the mullahs' Gestapo (Ministry of Intelligence), Khamenei's office and Hassan Rouhani on the terror list.

We urge you to set aside the policy of overlooking the main

> **Our people, our Resistance and the Mojahedin of Ashraf, have proven that they are prepared and ready to pay the price of freedom.**

force in Iranian society and history. Instead of complicity and shaking hands with the religious fascism, stand on the side of the people of Iran for regime change.

Then as Tony Blair wrote, "we will be astonished at how the challenge of extremism in the Middle East and beyond abates."

I specifically urge the new UK government to support human rights, namely the suppressed human rights of the people of Iran. I urge them to take action and to send an international fact-finding mission to Iran to visit the regime's prisons and the political prisoners, particularly women prisoners.

Baroness Boothroyd, former speaker of the House of Commons, once said that the massacre of political prisoners in

Iran in 1988, which took place after Khomeini was forced to accept the ceasefire in the (Iran-Iraq) war, has been the greatest crime against humanity since the Second World War. She said that no one has been held to account for this crime but there will come a day when we would witness the truth get rectified.

My fellow compatriots,

The ruling regime is surrounded by an impatient nation confident that her liberation will not be realized unless the mullahs are overthrown. The clerical regime has no more strength or resources and is struggling in a quagmire which will lead to its overthrow.

The era of religious fascism is coming to an end; Iran will be free. We will take back our most beautiful homeland by the resistance units and the Army of Freedom.

Hail to all of you.

www.ingramcontent.com/pod-product-compliance
Ingram Content Group UK Ltd.
Pitfield, Milton Keynes, MK11 3LW, UK
UKHW062313290726
14090UKWH00018B/1039